W9-DFG-017

RESCUING Animals FROM DISASTERS

SAVING ANIMALS AFTER EARTHQUAKES

by Joyce Markovics

Consultant: Dave Pauli
Senior Director, Wildlife Response
Humane Society of the United States
HSUS Animal Care Centers

BEARPORT
PUBLISHING

New York, New York

Credits

Cover and Title Page, © China Daily/Reuters/Landov and AFP/Getty Images; 4, © Yvan Travert/age fotostock; 5, © Franz Smets/EPA/Landov; 6, © David Sacks/The Image Bank/Getty Images; 7, © John Moore/Getty Images; 8, © Joe Raedle/Getty Images; 9L, © Brian Snyder/Reuters/Landov; 9R, © Ginny Dixon; 10, © Marco A. and Calvo F./IFAW-WSPA; 11, © IFAW-WSPA-RSPCA/T. Woodley; 12, © IFAW-WSPA/J.C. Bouvier; 13, © Kathy Milani/Humane Society International; 14, © Humane Society International; 15, © Julie Dermansky/Corbis; 16, © Kathy Milani/Humane Society International; 17, © Kathy Milani/Humane Society International; 18, © NaturePL/SuperStock; 19, © WENN/Newscom; 20, © AFP/Getty Images; 21L, © AP Photo/Kyodo News/Minoru Iwasaki; 21R, © AFP/Getty Images; 22, © EPA/Landov; 23, © Reuters/Landov; 24, © Imaginechina via AP Images; 25, © AP Photo/Andy Wong; 26, © AP Photo/Andy Wong; 27, © ZUMA Press/Newscom; 28, © Kyodo/Landov; 29, © Corbis/SuperStock.

Publisher: Kenn Goin
Senior Editor: Lisa Wiseman
Creative Director: Spencer Brinker
Design: Dawn Beard Creative and Kim Jones
Photo Researcher: Daniella Nilva

Library of Congress Cataloging-in-Publication Data

Markovics, Joyce L.
  Saving animals after earthquakes / by Joyce Markovics.
      p. cm. — (Rescuing animals from disasters)
  Includes bibliographical references and index.
  ISBN-13: 978-1-61772-289-9 (library binding)
  ISBN-10: 1-61772-289-8 (library binding)
  1. Animal rescue. 2. Animal welfare. 3. Disaster relief. I. Title.
  HV4708.M36 2012
  636.08'32—dc22
                                        2011005616

For more information, write to Bearport Publishing Company, Inc., 45 West 21st Street, Suite 3B, New York, New York 10010. Printed in the United States of America in North Mankato, Minnesota.

10 9 8 7 6 5 4 3 2 1

CONTENTS

Dashing for Cover

January 12, 2010, began as a quiet day in southern Haiti. Then, just before 5:00 P.M., the earth suddenly began to rumble and shake violently. Two small dogs named Bella and Deiter were inside their owner's third-floor apartment in the city of Port-au-Prince (*port*-oh-PRIHNS) when the huge **earthquake** struck. The terrified dogs scrambled for safety as **debris** rained down from the apartment's ceiling.

Port-au-Prince, Haiti's capital, before the massive earthquake

4

At the time of the massive quake, Paul Fowler, who owned Bella and Deiter, was outside the apartment building with his baby daughter, Victoria. "I saw the building swaying back and forth," Paul said. When the ground stopped shaking, there was debris and thick dust everywhere. Although badly damaged, the building remained standing. "It was like out of a movie set," Paul said about the destruction that surrounded him. "I thought for sure the dogs hadn't made it."

In about 40 seconds, the earthquake destroyed most of the buildings in and around Port-au-Prince.

The earthquake in Haiti was very strong, measuring 7.0 on the **Richter scale**. It was so powerful that people in parts of Cuba, more than 200 miles (322 km) away, felt it.

The country of Haiti is located on the island of Hispaniola in the Caribbean Sea.

A Bark for Help

With Victoria under one arm, Paul raced upstairs to find his apartment completely destroyed. As he stumbled over debris, he desperately called out for his dogs. However, there was no sign of them. Paul was about to give up his search when he heard a familiar bark. It was Deiter!

There were very few buildings that did not collapse during the quake.

The sound was coming from an area near a bed covered in **rubble**. Paul carefully picked through the dusty debris that covered the bed. When he had cleared the debris away, he saw that both dogs were hiding under the bed. They were frightened, but unharmed. "I think the bed saved them," Paul recalled. "They must have run under there when they first felt the earthquake." Still holding Victoria, Paul scooped up the two dogs with his other arm and walked out of the building.

After the earthquake, many people searched through rubble and debris looking for their loved ones and for their personal belongings.

More than 200,000 people lost their lives during the earthquake in Haiti. Nearly 300,000 homes were destroyed or damaged.

Rescued Twice

Amazingly, this was not the first time Deiter and Bella had survived a **natural disaster**. Before Paul and his family adopted the dogs, Deiter and Bella lived in separate homes in New Orleans. In 2005, both dogs were **abandoned** by their owners during Hurricane Katrina. Best Friends Animal Society, a group that works to help animals in need, rescued the dogs.

For about 250 days after Hurricane Katrina, Best Friends worked to save more than 4,000 homeless animals.

Best Friends saved thousands of animals during Hurricane Katrina, which led to the development of its Emergency Response Team. This special team leads animal rescue efforts around the world. In fact, a few weeks after the earthquake, Best Friends sent two members of the Emergency Response Team to Haiti to help out there.

Best Friends has sent its rescue team to Peru, the Philippines, and other areas hit hard by natural disasters. Here, a worker rescues a dog after Hurricane Katrina.

Paul Fowler with Dieter (left) and Bella (right)

When the Fowler family moved to Haiti after Hurricane Katrina, they brought Deiter and Bella with them.

9

On the Ground

In Haiti, the Emergency Response Team members joined the Animal Relief Coalition for Haiti (ARCH). This group had been created by the World Society for the Protection of Animals (WSPA) and the International Fund for Animal Welfare (IFAW) just days after the earthquake had occurred. Made up of **veterinarians**, animal handlers, and volunteers, ARCH's goal was to help animals in the hardest hit areas of the country.

More than 12 different **welfare** groups joined ARCH. In the first six months after the earthquake, ARCH gave medical care to about 25,000 animals.

An ARCH worker provides medical care to a cat.

Along with ARCH, the Emergency Response Team members set out to find and care for sick or injured animals. As they drove through the debris-clogged streets, they found mostly dogs and cats. Some had open wounds and broken bones. Since most of Haiti's buildings lay in ruins, the animals were treated on the streets where they had been found. The team bandaged wounds and operated on animals out in the open. ARCH also provided much-needed supplies, such as medicine and pet food, to help people care for their pets.

Rescue workers giving medical treatment to a dog on the street

Puppies in Need

Another organization that joined ARCH's rescue efforts in Haiti was the American Society for the Prevention of Cruelty to Animals (ASPCA). The ASPCA team, led by Jeff Eyre, helped save three hungry puppies inside the broken wall of a destroyed building. Although the puppies' mother was nearby, she wasn't able to take care of them. She was covered with cuts and bruises. She was also very skinny from lack of food and unable to produce enough milk to feed her puppies.

The puppies were removed from inside a wall and then examined for any sign of injury.

Members of the rescue team cleaned and wrapped the mother's wounds. They gave her an **antibiotic** so that the wounds would not get infected. Afterward, the team provided food and special medicine to the mother and her puppies to keep them healthy.

Stray dogs roaming the streets of Haiti after the earthquake

As many as 150,000 **stray** dogs were left to fend for themselves after the earthquake in Haiti.

Saving Farm Animals

In addition to dogs and cats, there were thousands of other animal victims in Haiti. The country is home to more than five million farm animals—mainly goats, cattle, sheep, pigs, and chickens, which Haitians depend on for food. Workers from the Humane Society of the United States (HSUS) and Humane Society International (HSI), animal protection organizations, set out to **assess** the overall condition of these animals.

A worker from the Humane Society rescue team (right) examines a donkey. Besides looking at the animals for injuries, the team taught Haitians how to properly care for their farm animals.

"Most of the animals were free-roaming, trying to survive on their own," said Dave Pauli, a director at the Humane Society of the United States. Farmers had freed these animals because they were unable to feed and take care of them after the quake. Some of the animals were searching for food in garbage dumps. The Humane Society rescue team brought food and medicine to these quake victims. "By helping the animals, we're helping the people," Dave said.

Hungry pigs search for food scraps after the earthquake.

The HSUS is the largest organization in the United States that protects and cares for animals in need of help around the world.

Long-term Care

Just weeks after the earthquake, the Humane Society rescue team set up a variety of programs to help care for Haiti's animals. They put together special kits for local veterinarians to use to treat sick or injured animals in the countryside. The kits included bandages, antibiotics, and other medicine. In addition, they organized a long-term program to **vaccinate** all stray dogs, cats, and other animals against deadly diseases such as **rabies**.

A veterinarian with the Humane Society rescue team examines a dog.

Even before the disaster, there were no animal shelters or groups in Haiti to help animals in need. So the Humane Society rescue team worked with the Haitian government to set up animal welfare programs and to build Haiti's first animal care center.

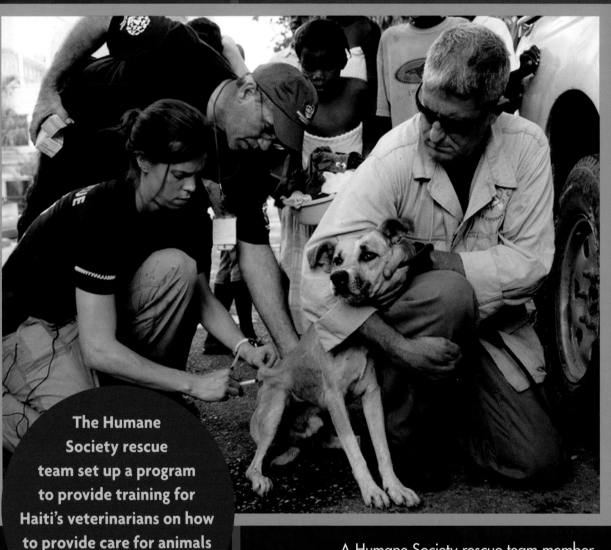

The Humane Society rescue team set up a program to provide training for Haiti's veterinarians on how to provide care for animals during a natural disaster.

A Humane Society rescue team member gently holds a dog while a veterinarian gives the animal a vitamin shot.

Panda-monium in China

Earthquakes have also affected animals in other parts of the world. In May 2008, a huge earthquake hit Sichuan (SECH-won) province in southwest China. The Wolong National Nature **Reserve**, home to many **endangered** giant pandas, was badly damaged.

Before the earthquake, these pandas lived peacefully in the mountains of the Wolong Nature Reserve.

When the earthquake hit, large rocks were **dislodged** from the mountains surrounding the reserve. "These rocks were just flying in the air," recalled Walter Weber, who was visiting the area when the quake struck. The huge rocks destroyed parts of the reserve, including some of the areas where the adult and baby pandas lived. Some of the adult pandas tried to run to higher ground, while a number of the babies darted up trees or poles and huddled together for safety.

Landslides within the reserve buried much of the bamboo that the pandas eat as their main food source.

The Wolong Nature Reserve, an important **refuge** for pandas, was only 20 miles (32 km) from the **epicenter** of the quake.

Up a Tree

When rescuers reached the reserve minutes after the quake, they found destruction everywhere. While the baby pandas appeared unharmed, some of them would not come down from their **perches**. Many were shaking with fear. The rescuers patiently **coaxed** each panda down. Then the babies were carefully carried, one by one, to safety and checked for injuries.

Pandas being coaxed down from their perch

Some of the adults were not so lucky. A nine-year-old panda named Mao Mao was crushed to death by falling debris inside her **pen**. Another adult panda died from his injuries shortly after he was rescued from the quake.

This injured panda was found alive and carried to safety by rescuers.

Workers feeding the pandas after the earthquake

There are only about 1,600 giant pandas living in the wild. They live high in the mountains in central China. No one knows for sure how many wild pandas the earthquake affected.

A Dog's Best Friend

The earthquake in China also devastated the area around the city of Chengdu, the capital of Sichuan province. Chen Yunlian, who runs an animal shelter, was determined to help as many four-legged survivors as she could.

The 2008 earthquake caused widespread destruction in western China. Nearly 70,000 people died.

For more than ten years, Chen, a former businesswoman, has run an animal shelter near Chengdu, where she cares for injured and homeless dogs and cats.

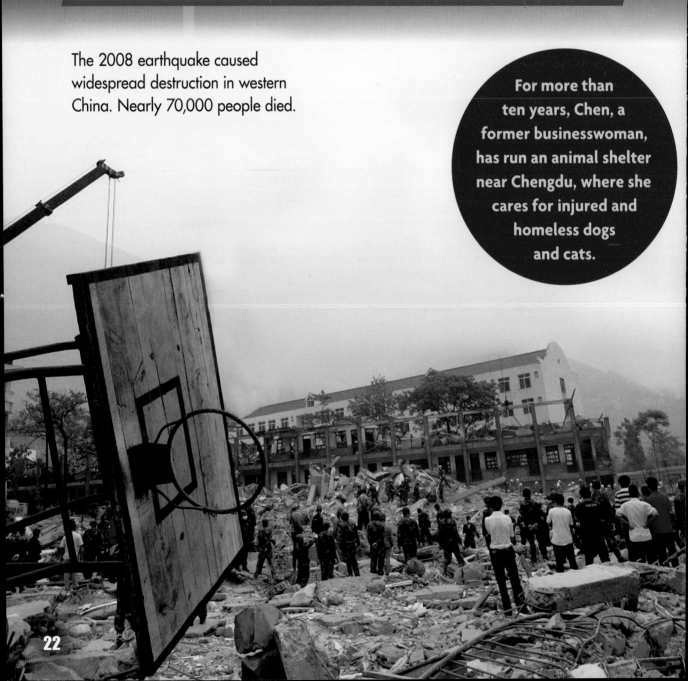

In the weeks following the quake, Chen drove around in a van to the worst hit areas. She searched the streets and rubble for trapped, hurt, and homeless animals. She also asked local people if they knew any animals in need of help. Chen found many survivors, including one dog dragging his crushed back legs through the dust and debris. She carefully placed the dog in her van and drove him back to her shelter for treatment.

Chen Yunlian at her animal shelter feeding the
dogs she found after the earthquake

Lending a Paw

Chen and a team of volunteers also found **canine** survivors near Pengzhou, a city in Sichuan province. Two dogs named Qianjin and Guai Guai had stayed with their owner as she lay trapped under a collapsed building. For more than eight days, the dogs remained with her. "Every day, they stayed by her side and licked her lips and face when she was thirsty," said Chen.

Chen and Qianjin

When rescuers finally reached the woman, the dogs barked loudly so that the rescuers could find her and pull her to safety. Chen took both furry heroes back to her shelter until their owner was able to recover and rebuild her home.

In Chinese, *Qianjin* means "forge ahead" and *Guai Guai* means "well behaved."

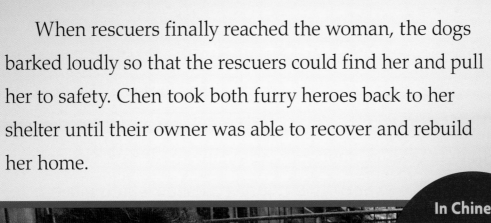

Qianjin (right), a small yellow dog, and Guai Guai (left), a Sheltie, were both in good health when they were rescued.

Quake Dogs

Back at her shelter, known as the "House of Love," Chen fed and cared for Qianjin and Guai Guai and the other injured dogs she had rescued. Many of the animals had broken bones and other injuries caused by falling debris that made it difficult or impossible for them to walk.

Chen examines an injured dog that was rescued after the earthquake.

In total, Chen's team rescued more than 100 dogs affected by the earthquake.

For the dogs that had been **crippled** by their injuries, Chen made special carts so that they could get around on their own. The carts were made from lightweight plastic pipes and wheels. "I think that dogs and humans have the same right to live," said Chen as she cuddled with a dog that had only three legs.

Like Chen, hundreds of other animal rescuers have dedicated their lives to saving animals from natural disasters. To them, all earthquake survivors deserve a helping hand.

The special carts made it easier for the injured dogs to move around.

FAMOUS EARTHQUAKES AND RESCUES

Rescue workers have learned a lot from rescuing animals after earthquakes. Here are two other quakes that put animals in danger.

Japan Earthquake, 2011
- The March 11, 2011, earthquake that hit Japan measured 8.9 on the Richter scale. The earthquake and the tsunami that soon followed left millions of people and animals, including cats and dogs, without homes, food, or water.
- Shortly after the quake and tsunami hit, the Japan Earthquake Animal Rescue and Support group (JEARS) was created. Workers from the group searched on foot for lost, trapped, and abandoned animals. They brought pet supplies to shelters where people and their pets were staying. They also took in pets that people were no longer able to care for.

A dog being brought to safety after the earthquake in Japan

Costa Rica Earthquake, 2009
- The earthquake that hit Costa Rica on January 8, 2009, destroyed roads, buildings, and caused landslides. Many owners were forced to abandon their pets as they tried to escape the **devastation**.
- Lighthouse Animal Rescue was one of the first rescue organizations in the area after the quake hit. They brought sacks of food, water, and medical supplies to trapped or hurt animals. The animals that the rescue group helped included dogs, cats, parrots, goats, pigs, and a newborn calf.

ANIMALS AT RISK FROM EARTHQUAKES

Earthquakes are dangerous natural disasters that can affect different animals in different ways.

Pets

- Pets can be killed or trapped in homes that collapse after an earthquake. Unlike many other places in the world, pet owners in Haiti often allow their pets to wander outside their homes. As a result, many pets did not become trapped by falling buildings and survived the 2010 earthquake.

- There is often very little food or clean water available after an earthquake, causing many lost or abandoned pets to die from hunger or thirst.

- Pet owners who live in areas where earthquakes occur should make sure their pets wear name tags. They should also have recent photos of their pets in case they get separated during an earthquake.

- The best way to protect pets during an earthquake is for owners to take the animals with them when they evacuate.

Wildlife

- Earthquakes can destroy animal **habitats**, forcing animals to live in smaller areas. This may cause their **population** to decrease.

- According to some experts, wildlife such as giant pandas and elephants can sense an earthquake before it strikes. These experts believe that the animals have a special ability to feel small changes in the environment that can signal earthquakes. The animals may react by becoming restless or moving to higher ground.

Before the 2008 earthquake in China, visitors at the Wolong Nature Reserve saw the pandas acting strangely. One visitor noticed that the pandas suddenly went from being "really lazy" to "parading around their pen."

GLOSSARY

abandoned (uh-BAN-duhnd) left alone and uncared for; deserted

antibiotic (*an*-ti-bye-OT-ik) medicine used to destroy or stop the growth of bacteria that cause disease

assess (uh-SESS) to judge how good or bad something is

canine (KAY-nine) a member of the dog family

coaxed (KOHKST) gently persuaded to do something

crippled (KRIP-uhld) disabled, or not able to walk due to injury

debris (duh-BREE) scattered pieces of something that has been wrecked or destroyed

devastation (*dev*-uh-STAY-shuhn) massive destruction caused by the action of people or of nature

dislodged (diss-LOJD) forced out of position

earthquake (URTH-*kwayk*) a sudden shaking of the ground caused by the moving of Earth's outer layer

endangered (en-DAYN-jurd) being in danger of dying out

epicenter (EP-uh-*sent*-ur) the area of land above where an earthquake occurs

habitats (HAB-uh-*tats*) places in nature where plants or animals normally live

natural disaster (NACH-ur-uhl duh-ZASS-tur) an event such as an earthquake or tsunami that is caused by nature rather than people

pen (PEN) a small, enclosed area for animals, such as pigs, sheep, and cows

perches (PURCH-iz) places above the ground where people or animals can sit or stand

population (*pop*-yuh-LAY-shuhn) the number of people or animals living in a place

rabies (RAY-beez) an often deadly disease spread by the bite of an infected animal

refuge (REF-yooj) a place that protects animals or people

reserve (ri-SURV) a protected place where animals can live safely

Richter scale (RIHK-tuhr SKALE) a number system used to indicate the strength of earthquakes; the higher the number, the more powerful the earthquake

rubble (RUHB-uhl) broken pieces of rock, brick, concrete, and other building materials

stray (STRAY) a lost or homeless cat or dog

vaccinate (VAK-suh-nate) to protect a person or animal against a disease by giving the person or animal a special shot

veterinarians (*vet*-ur-uh-NER-ee-uhnz) doctors who take care of dogs and other animals

welfare (WEL-fair) having to do with the well-being of a person or animal

BIBLIOGRAPHY

Kuhn, Anthony. "After Earthquake, Animal Lovers to the Rescue." All Things Considered, National Public Radio (May 30, 2008).

Peters, Sharon L. "Lucky Dogs Rescued After Katrina, Now Haiti." *USA Today* (January 27, 2010).

The American Society for the Prevention of Cruelty to Animals:
www.aspca.org

Best Friends Animal Society:
network.bestfriends.org/golocal/international/14332/news.aspx

The Humane Society of the United States:
www.humanesociety.org/news/haiti_disaster_response.html

READ MORE

Aronin, Miriam. *Earthquake in Haiti (Code Red).* New York: Bearport (2011).

Best Friends Animal Society. *Not Left Behind: Rescuing the Pets of New Orleans.* New York: Yorkville Press (2006).

Fradin, Judy and Dennis. *Witness to Disaster: Earthquakes.* Washington, D.C.: National Geographic Children's Books (2008).

LEARN MORE ONLINE

To learn more about saving animals after earthquakes, visit
www.bearportpublishing.com/RescuingAnimalsfromDisasters

INDEX

ABOUT THE AUTHOR

Joyce Markovics is an editor, writer, and orchid collector. She encourages anyone looking for a pet to consider adopting one of the many homeless animals living in shelters across the United States.